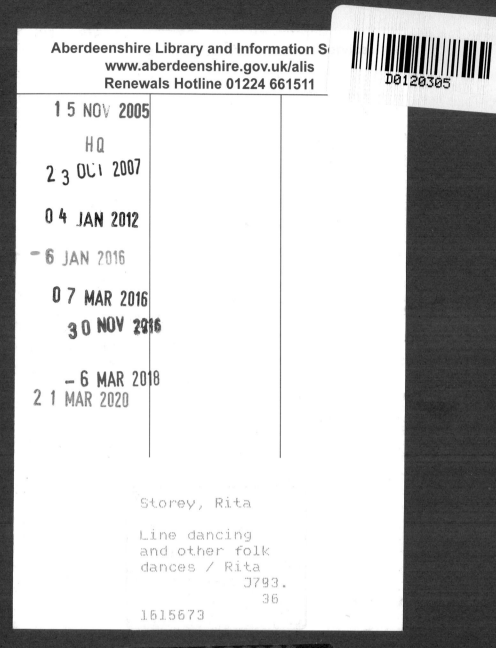

LINE DANCING

AND OTHER FOLK DANCES

RITA STOREY

W

FRANKLIN WATTS
LONDON • SYDNEY

LINE DANCING

AND OTHER FOLK DANCES

Folk dances were created by ordinary working people, or peasants, and passed on from one generation to the next. The style of folk dancing was different to the more genteel dances of the upper classes.

Folk dances were often performed to celebrate important events such as a marriage, or a religious ceremony. Many folk dances have been lost over the years. Nowadays, folk dance tends to be performed by small, specialist groups for audiences of tourists, rather than by whole communities.

Line dancing is a modern version of American folk dancing. It is very popular in the USA and has spread to other countries too. Dancers step out to country and western music.

Why should *I* dance?

Dancing is good for everyone. It's a great way to get fit. All types of dancing are a form of aerobic exercise, which encourages your heart and lungs to work hard. Over time, this will help them to become stronger and make *you* fitter.

The food we eat provides our body with the energy it needs to work properly. But if we eat more calories than our body needs, these are stored as fat. Dancing makes your body burn off calories. Your muscles will strengthen and become firmer, and your body will become more shapely.

Dancing makes you happy

When you take exercise, your brain makes a hormone called seratonin, which makes you feel happy. So if you're feeling miserable, put down the chocolate, put on the music and start dancing.

There are so many types of dance that there really is something for everyone. You can do the dance moves in this book on your own or with a friend, and work at a pace that suits you.

Dancing can even boost your brain power. Putting together dance steps increases your coordination and helps keep your mind alert.

Last but not least, dancing is fun. So what are you waiting for? Turn up the music and get moving!

Contents

Let's get moving 4
Warm-up exercises to do before you start.

Cool it! 7
How to cool down after a dance session.

Line dancing 8
What is line dancing all about?

Boot scootin' steps 10
Learn some line dance steps and show your boots how to scoot.

The electric slide 14
Put steps together and dance a complete line dance.

Ceilidh dancing 17
Learn an English, a Scottish and an Irish ceilidh dance.

Hungarian folk dance 24
Practise some traditional Hungarian folk dance steps.

Special folk dances 28
Find out about the special meanings of some dances.

Further information 30

Glossary 31

Index 32

Let's get moving

Why do I have to warm up?

Before you learn any new dance steps and begin to put them together, it is important to warm up your muscles to prevent cramp and muscle strain. You may only be able to do the exercises a couple of times to start with, but persevere and do a few more repeats each time. A warm-up should last about ten minutes.

There are warm-up moves in each of the four books in the Get Dancing series. You can combine them to make a routine.

Aerobic exercises

The first set of exercises is aerobic, which means that it improves your breathing and circulation. Aerobic exercise increases your oxygen intake by making your heart beat faster. To do it, you have to keep on the move all the time. Each set of aerobic exercises is designed to be repeated. If you are not used to exercise and feel your pulse starting to race, stop and jog on the spot to keep warm.

AEROBIC EXERCISE
JUMPING JACKS

1 Hold your arms out at right angles to the ground, with your elbows bent.

2 Jump in the air, making a star shape with your arms and legs.

3 Jump back to position 1.

Repeat 5 times.

ISOLATION

SHOULDER ISOLATION

1 Hold your arms straight out to the side. Keeping your shoulders square to the front, stretch your right arm and shoulder as far to the right as you can.

2 Keeping your shoulders square, stretch your left arm and shoulder as far to the left as you can.

Repeat 4 times to each side.

Body isolations

The second set of exercises is a body isolation. This type of exercise teaches you to move parts of your body individually, which is important for any type of dancing.

What to wear

Wear something comfortable to do a warm-up, such as loose-fitting trousers (not jeans), a T-shirt, and a loose, long-sleeved top that you can take off when you have warmed up.

You can do the routine in bare feet, trainers or jazz shoes. Don't do it in socks, or you may slip.

Dance to the music

You will need at least two pieces of music for the warm-up. The first is for the aerobic exercises. It should be energetic and upbeat, to make everyone feel enthusiastic. It can also be used for body isolations, which are sharp, quick moves.

The second piece of music will be used for the stretches and toning exercises (see page 6). Gentle, relaxing music is best for this part of the warm-up.

5

Stretches

The most important thing to remember about stretches is that they should be done gradually. It's easy to pull a muscle by pushing yourself too hard, too soon.

Try doing the exercises every day and stretching just a little bit further each time. If it hurts, STOP. You may feel a bit stiff the next day if you haven't been exercising regularly, but you shouldn't be in pain. If you are, you have stretched too hard – stop for a few days and then start building up the stretches slowly.

Toning exercises

These exercises are to strengthen and tone particular muscles, giving you a better body shape and strong muscles to hold the dance moves.

STRETCH AND TONE
PLIÉS

1 Stand with your feet apart, toes pointing outwards. Keeping your back straight, bend your knees and gently lower your body as low as you can.

2 Straighten your knees and rise up on to your toes, and then lower yourself down gently. (You can hold on to the back of a chair to help you balance.)

Repeat 5 times.

Cool it!

At the end of a dance session, it is important to do a cool-down routine to help prevent stiffness the next day. The routine concentrates on stretching exercises that stretch out and relax the muscles. To be effective, each stretch should be held for a slow count of ten. A cool-down routine should last for five to ten minutes.

Each of the four books in the Get Dancing series contains cool-down stretches. You can use a combination from different books if you wish.

Hold each move for a slow count of 10.

COOL IT! 1
LEG STRETCH

1 Standing up straight, bend your right leg tightly against your body. Tilt your hips forward to increase the stretch. (If you wish, you can hold on to something with your free hand.) Repeat with your left leg.

COOL IT! 2
SIDE STRETCH

1 Stand with your feet slightly apart. Without twisting your body, stretch your arm up and over your head to the side, stretching as far as you can.

2 Repeat on the other side.

7

Line dancing

Line dancing comes from America. As the name suggests, line dancing is danced in lines. Girls and boys dance the same steps at the same time, and everyone starts and finishes together.

The steps

Line dances are built up of groups of steps, which appear in lots of different dances. Once you have mastered the basic steps, the number of combinations you can dance is endless.

The counts

Each dance is made up of a sequence of different moves, which are called 'counts'.

Turning

Each set of steps is usually danced four times, with a quarter-turn (90°) between each set. You dance each set of steps to each of the four walls in the room and finish back where you started. In more advanced line dancing, the steps might be done with a half-turn (180°) between them instead. It is important to remember which wall you should be facing, however the dance is done!

Hands

Apart from doing an occasional clap, your hands are not very important in a line dancing routine. To look like an American line dancer, tuck your thumbs into your belt, belt loops or the pockets of your jeans as you perform the steps.

What to wear

Line dancing clothes are very casual and, as you might expect for an American folk dance, they follow a cowboy theme.

Both girls and boys usually wear jeans or cords with a belt that they can tuck their thumbs into. Footwear consists of cowboy boots or sturdy, low-heeled shoes. (Trainers are no good as they grip the floor and make doing turns difficult. They can also squeak when you turn!) A T-shirt or shirt and a cowboy hat complete the outfit.

Outfits with fringes that swing as you turn can look very effective.

THE STORY OF AMERICAN LINE DANCING

In America in the 1800s, there was a very popular style of folk dancing called contra dancing. Two lines of dancers faced each other as they danced the steps. (Contra dancing evolved into square dancing, which is similar to English barn dancing.)

Country and western

As migrant workers arrived in America from Germany and other European countries, they brought folk dances with them. A new dancing style was born, which was a mixture of contra dancing and European dancing. It became known as country and western. In the 1930s, as more and more people got radios, there was a huge increase in the popularity of country and western music.

In the 1980s, a film called *Urban Cowboy*, which starred John Travolta, brought country and western to a mass audience and helped to make it even more popular.

Line dancing

Line dancing has its roots in contra dancing and many of the steps are the same. But in line dancing you don't need a partner, whereas in contra dancing you do. Contra steps called scuffs, hitches and hooks are used in modern line dancing.

'Achey Breaky Heart'

The popularity of line dancing and country and western music soared in the 1990s after a singer called Billy Ray Cyrus released a record called 'Achey Breaky Heart'. In the UK, many people thought that line dancing looked fun and wanted to try it, and so line dancing classes opened all over the country.

A caller sings out the dance moves at an American square dance.

Boot scootin' steps

Line dances are made up of a series of basic steps put together in different combinations. Steps 1 to 9, shown on pages 10–13, are basic steps. When you have practised these, see if you can make up your own dance sequence. To line dance with real country and western style, dip your shoulders and sway your hips as you move sideways. Your boots will scoot across the floor – which is how boot scootin' steps get their name!

Dance to the music

Various Artists: *Boot Scootin' Fever*. Various Artists: *Line Dance Fever 8–15*. Various Artists: *Country Line Dancing*. Various Artists: *The Best Line Dancing Album in the World... Ever*. Billy Ray Cyrus: *The Definitive Collection*.

STEP 1
GRAPEVINE

1 Step out to the left.

2 Step your right foot behind your left foot.

3 Step out to the left.

4 Step together and clap.

VARIATION
A grapevine can also be done to the right.
A grapevine move can be finished with a hitch step,
or a scuff (see opposite) instead of a clap.

THE DANCE RANCH

A 'dance ranch' is a venue holding a country and western dance party. In the 1980s, dance ranches sprang up all over the United States. People who went to the USA on holiday discovered that it was fun to go to a dance ranch, and the trend began to spread throughout the world.

Dance ranches were popular because no one needed a partner, it didn't matter what you wore, and the music was great to dance to. Often, there was a caller to shout out the moves, so it wasn't even necessary to know the order of the steps. This made the dances ideal for all ages and abilities.

STEP **2**
HITCH STEP

Bring one knee up, keeping your foot parallel to the floor. Step it down alongside the foot you are standing on.

STEP **3**
SCUFF STEP

Kick your foot forward, scuffing the floor and ending with the foot stretched out. Then put it back alongside your other foot.

STEP **4**
BOOT SCOOT

Scuff one foot forwards, then bring your knee up and hop on the back foot. Put your raised foot down alongside the other foot.

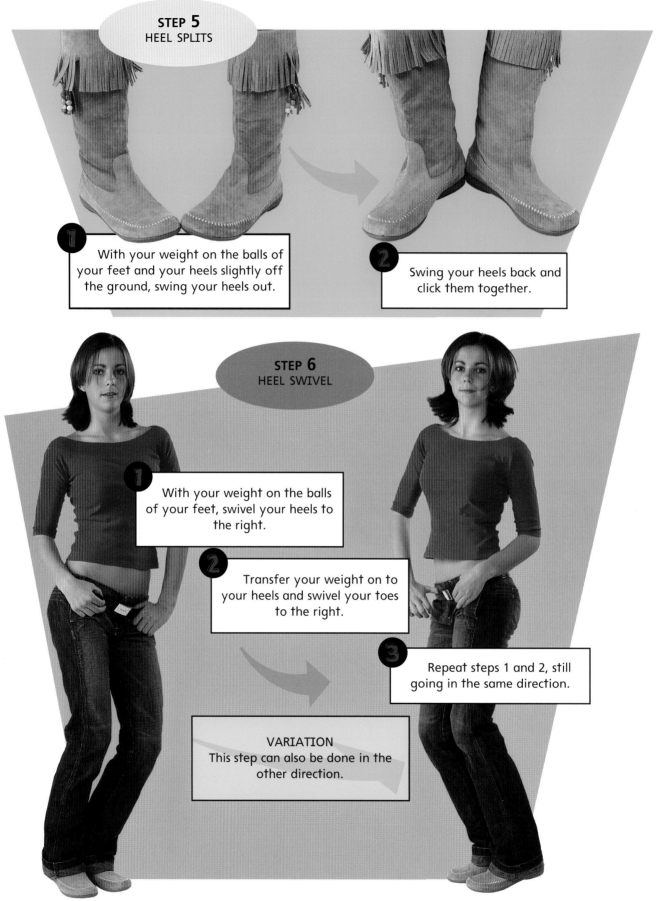

STEP 5
HEEL SPLITS

1 With your weight on the balls of your feet and your heels slightly off the ground, swing your heels out.

2 Swing your heels back and click them together.

STEP 6
HEEL SWIVEL

1 With your weight on the balls of your feet, swivel your heels to the right.

2 Transfer your weight on to your heels and swivel your toes to the right.

3 Repeat steps 1 and 2, still going in the same direction.

VARIATION
This step can also be done in the other direction.

STEP 7
TOE TAP

STEP 8
HOOK STEP

STEP 9
HEEL DIG

Tap your toe on the ground without transferring any weight on to it.
Put your foot back down again.
This step can be done in front or behind.

Tap the heel of your foot on the ground.
Put your foot back down again.

Lift your leg and place the heel of your foot in front of the leg you are standing on, at shin height.
Put your foot back down again.

VARIATION
A hook step can be done with either leg, to the front or to the back.

The electric slide

The electric slide is a popular line dance, in which you dance the same sequence of steps in four directions. The dance has eighteen counts. You dance the eighteen-step sequence

shown below and finish by doing a quarter-turn to the left. By dancing the sequence four times, once to each wall in the room, you will get back to where you started.

1 (Steps 1–4 are a grapevine to the right.)
Step out to the right.

2 Cross your left foot behind your right foot.

3 Step out to the right.

4 Bring your left foot next to your right foot and clap.

5–8 (Steps 5–8 are a grapevine to the left.)
5. Step out to the left.
6. Cross your right foot behind your left foot.
7. Step out to the left.
8. Bring your right foot next to your left foot and clap.

14

10 Step back on the left foot.

9 Step back on the right foot.

11 Step back on the right foot.

12 Touch your left foot beside your right foot.

13 Step forward on the left foot.

14 Touch your right foot beside your left foot, without transferring your weight on to this foot.

Continued on page 16

The electric slide

15 Step back on the right foot.

16 Touch your left foot in front of your right foot, without transferring your weight on to this foot.

17 Step forward on the left foot.

18a Kick your right foot forward, scuffing the floor. Turn at the same time, swivelling your left foot to make a quarter-turn to the left.

18b Put your right foot down next to your left foot. Start again at the beginning.

Dance to the music

Various Artists: *Christy Lane's Line Dancing Music* – 'Boot Scootin' Boogie'.
Marcia Griffiths: 'Electric Boogie'.

Ceilidh dancing

SCOTTISH, IRISH AND ENGLISH CEILIDH DANCES

What is a ceilidh?

The word 'ceilidh' (which is pronounced 'kaylee') means 'an informal gathering'. Ceilidhs are held throughout Europe, but especially in rural communities in Scotland, Ireland (where they are known as 'ceilis'), and parts of England and Wales.

History of the ceilidh

In its early history, the ceilidh was a tradition of working people, or peasants. Ceilidhs were held a few times a year. At a ceilidh, neighbours would gather together for an evening of dancing, singing and storytelling. Ceilidhs have helped to make sure that traditional folk dances, songs and stories have not been forgotten.

The music

Ceilidhs often have a caller to shout out the dance steps and walk the dancers through the moves. Music is played on traditional instruments such as fiddles, whistles, bodrans (hand-held drums played with a stick), harps, banjos, guitars, flutes, accordions and even spoons. The dances include jigs, reels, hornpipes and polkas, and are very energetic. There is often a pause between dances, for a song or two, so that people can get their breath back.

Dance to the music

Footnotes: *The Complete Scottish Ceilidh Dance* (contains music for the gay gordons and the Saint Bernard's waltz). Matt Cunningham: *15 Ceili Dances* (contains music for the bridge of Athlone). The Marwicks: *Ceilidh Sets* (contains music for the gay gordons). Star Accordion Band: *Scottish Dance Favourites* (contains music for the Saint Bernard's waltz).

At a ceilidh, people dance to music played live on traditional instruments.

Ceilidh dancing

An English ceilidh dance

The Saint Bernard's waltz is a popular English ceilidh dance. This dance is done in pairs. Couples make a circle around the room, with the girls on the outside and the boys on the inside. Everybody moves anticlockwise.

THE SAINT BERNARD'S WALTZ

Ballroom hold
For this dance, use the ballroom hold. The girl puts her left hand on the boy's right shoulder and holds his left hand with her right hand. The boy puts his right hand on the girl's waist and holds her right hand with his left hand.

1 Take three steps sideways towards the girl's right and stamp both feet.
Counts: one; two; three; stamp, stamp (four).

2 Take two steps back the other way.
Counts: one, two.

3 Take two steps towards the centre of the room.
Counts: one, two.
(The girl goes forwards, right, then left; the boy goes backwards, left, then right.)

4 Take two steps towards the outside of the room, using the same movements as in step 3.
Counts: one, two.

⑤ The girl turns on the spot under the boy's raised arm. Counts: one, two.

⑥ Go back to a ballroom hold and sidestep to the girl's right for four beats. Counts: one, two, three, four. Start again at the beginning.

ENGLISH DANCES

Modern English ceilidh dances
These are very similar to barn dances, a type of dance that is popular in England. Both are energetic folk dances, which have a caller to guide people through the dance moves.

English country dancing
In eighteenth-century England, peasants had ceilidhs, but better educated and wealthier people had a more formal style of dancing. Their dances became known as English country dancing.

Ceilidh dancing

A Scottish ceilidh dance
The gay gordons is a popular dance. It is thought that it got its name from a Scottish regiment, the Gordon Highlanders, who wore bright uniforms. This dance is done in pairs.

THE GAY GORDONS

Position for the gay gordons
All the couples make a circle, with the girls on the outside. Everyone faces anticlockwise.

Hold for the gay gordons
With his right hand, the boy holds his partner's right hand behind her right shoulder (high position). He holds her left hand in his left hand, in front of his waist (low position).

1 Start on the right foot. Walk forwards four steps, turning 180° as you do so, to face the opposite way. As you turn, move your left arm into the high position and your right arm into the low position (see step 2).
Counts: one, two, three, four.

2 Do exactly the same as in step 1, but going the other way.
Counts: one, two, three, four.

What to wear
There are no rules about what to wear to a ceilidh – almost anything goes. Remember that if you are going to be dancing all evening, you need to wear clothes that will keep you cool, and some comfortable shoes.

3 The boy turns the girl under his raised arm for four beats. Counts: one, two, three, four.

4 Change to a ballroom hold (see page 18) and sidestep for four beats. Counts: one, two, three, four. Start again at the beginning.

SCOTTISH DANCES

Scottish ceilidh dancing

Ceilidhs are held throughout the year and also to celebrate special occasions such as New Year (which is known as Hogmanay) and Burns Night, which celebrates the Scottish poet Robert Burns. They are usually very lively! The dances are very informal.

Scottish country dancing

Scottish country dances are more complicated and elegant than those performed at a ceilidh. Traditionally, girls wear long, white dresses with tartan sashes, and boys wear kilts, fitted black jackets with polished metal buttons, and long socks.

Ceilidh dancing

An Irish ceili dance

The bridge of Athlone is an Irish ceili dance. It is a dance for five couples.

The girls stand in a line holding hands. The boys also stand in a line holding hands, facing the girls.

THE BRIDGE OF ATHLONE

Both lines walk forward four steps and back four steps.

The boys turn to face each other and hold their hands up to make arches; the girls skip under and turn to face their partners.

Both lines walk forward four steps and back four steps.

The girls turn to face each other and hold their hands up to make arches; the boys skip under and turn to face their partners.

The leading couple (at the top of the line) join hands and gallop down between the lines and back again.

The leading couple skip down the outside of the lines; everyone else follows.

The leading couple stop at the bottom of the lines and make an arch. Everyone else goes through it back to where they started. The leading couple stay at the bottom of the line.

Everybody makes an arch. The lead girl goes up through the arches and back down the outside; at the same time the lead boy goes up the outside of the line, then back down through the arches. Once again, the leading couple end up at the bottom of the line.

Everyone swings their partner. Repeat the sequence, with the new leading couple at the top of the line taking the lead.

IRISH DANCES

Ceili dancing
This is the folk dancing of Ireland and can be done in lines, circles or squares. It is very different from step dancing.

Step dancing
This is danced on the toes, and includes high kicks and jumps (as seen in the popular musical, *Riverdance*).

Hungarian folk dance

Hungary has many different types of folk dance. Pages 24–27 give you a taster of some typical dance steps.

Pages 24–27

HEEL CLICK

What to wear

When they are performing, Hungarian dancers often wear clothes in the colours of the Hungarian flag: red, white and green. Women usually wear a full skirt, a blouse, and a jacket decorated with ribbons or embroidery. Men wear black or white trousers, a shirt, and a waistcoat covered with elaborate decoration.

1 Stand with your left hand on your hip.
Raise your right hand in the air, with the palm and fingers facing outwards.
Put your knees together and swing your heels out to the side.

2 Twist your hand so that the palm faces inwards; at the same time, click your heels together.

EUROPEAN FOLK DANCING

There is a lively tradition of folk dancing throughout Europe. In many places, traditional dances have not been forgotten and have been kept very much alive. They are danced in the villages by young and old alike.

Hungarian harvest dance

In Hungary in the autumn, a special dance is performed to celebrate the harvest. Fruit is suspended above the dancers' heads, and at the end of the dance, dancers are encouraged to steal the fruit.

The tarantella

This dance comes from southern Italy. It is performed with tambourines and castanets. A story claims that the tarantula spider was named after the dance. The story goes that a man was bitten by a poisonous spider. To save his life, the man danced and danced while the townspeople played music. He survived, and the poisonous spider was renamed the tarantula.

The zorba

Greek men traditionally perform the zorba. Everyone stands in a line with their hands on each other's shoulders, and dances a slow series of steps called a *hassapiko*. This involves making crossover steps whilst bending at the knee. The dance gets faster and faster, and the knee bends get lower and lower, as the dance progresses.

The mazurka

This Polish dance is very difficult to learn. Originally it was a dance where only the very basic steps were taught, and every dancer created new steps and variations.

The Cossack dance

The Cossack dance comes from Ukraine and was originally performed by soldiers. It is a very energetic dance where the dancer crouches down, with his arms crossed or outstretched, and kicks out his legs to the front while spinning around.

Greek men performing the zorba dance.

Hungarian folk dance

1 Stand with your left hand on your hip. Raise your right hand in the air with the palm and fingers facing outwards. Put your weight on your right foot and lift your left foot up behind you with the knee bent.

2 Step on to your back (left) foot and transfer your weight to it, slightly bending the knee. As you do so, move your foot round so that you turn slightly to the right.

3 Step on to your front (right) foot again, bending the knee slightly. As you do so, move your front foot so that you turn more to the right.

4 Repeat these moves, turning in a full circle. Dance the moves with your back straight, your shoulders pulled back, and your head held high.

VARIATION
You can do the same move turning anticlockwise, starting step 1 by putting your left hand in the air and your right foot behind.

HUNGARIAN RHYTHM
STEP 2

1 Stand on your left foot, with your right leg bent at the knee.
Put your left hand on your hip.
Bring your right hand up to chest height, and turn your wrist in towards your body so that your palm and fingers are facing upwards.

2 Kick your right leg forwards, tapping the heel on the floor. Sweep your right hand down and out to the side, keeping the palm facing up.

Dance to the music

Living Village Music (Volumes 1–9): *Traditional Hungarian Folk Music.* Kati Szvorák and Köfaragók: *Meotis.*

3 Hop back on to your left leg and put both hands on your hips.
Place your right foot down by your left.
Repeat the sequence, using the opposite foot and hand.

Special folk dances

Folk dances, made up and performed by ordinary people, exist all over the world. Because folk dances are handed down from one generation to another, it is easy for them to be lost, especially if people have to move away from their homeland for any reason.

But sometimes people took their traditional dances with them when they moved to another country. As people settled into their new communities, their folk dances often became blended with the folk dances of the new country. It is not surprising that today we often find the same dance steps in different countries and in various styles of dance.

Dances to show emotion
Some folk dances were used to express a range of different emotions. Sometimes people wanted to show that they were happy, or sad about a loss. Sometimes they wanted to express gratitude for a good harvest or the birth of a healthy child. Sometimes dances were performed to bring luck and prosperity. Native Americans used to perform a buffalo dance to thank the gods for buffaloes, which were a source of food and clothing.

Performance dances
Certain folk dances were devised to be performed by semi-professional groups and watched (rather than danced) by everyone. English morris dancing is an example of this.

Morris dancing
You can still watch morris dancing today. This very energetic form of dancing is done by teams of people dressed in traditional costume.

A high-skipping morris dancer wearing traditional leg bells.

The dances and the costumes vary from county to county. In some places, dancers wave hankderchiefs as they dance; others use sticks to stage mock fights.

Morris dances were originally performed on special occasions. For example, dances took place at the beginning of spring, to ensure that crops would grow well and there would be a good harvest.

Telling a story

Folk dancing has also traditionally been used to tell a story. The stories often had a moral, such as good triumphing over evil. In southern India, there are dances depicting mythical and religious stories, such as the triumph of the god Krishna over a giant evil serpent called Kaliya.

Sometimes, dances were a way of passing on traditional tales and the history of a people from one generation to another. The Polynesian people of Hawaii used to teach their children about the history of Hawaii through hula dances.

Dancing away the spirits

In some cultures, dancing is a way of getting rid of evil spirits and getting closer to God. Sufi Muslims in Turkey have dancers called whirling dervishes, who perform spectacular spinning dances to pass on God's blessing to onlookers.

In modern Hawaii, hula dancing is danced to express happiness.

Further information

Websites

www.linedancelessons.com
Step-by-step instructions for six dances for free; many more available to buy.

bbc.co.uk/scotland/musicscotland/celticroots
Step-by-step instructions and animated feet show how to do the gay gordons and military two-step.

www.rad.org.uk
Royal Academy of Dance.
The Royal Academy runs schools throughout the UK; the syllabus includes dance from Hungary, Russia and Poland.

Videos and DVDs

Let's Dance – Step in Line
Line dancing for beginners (video).

Step We Ceilidh
Learn how to perform thirteen popular ceilidh dances including the eightsome reel, the lancers, gay gordons, circle waltz, pride of Erin and highland fair (video).

Let's Dance: Barn Dancing Step by Step
This step-by-step guide will make sure that you are well prepared for any barn dance you attend (video).

Ceili Dancing Step by Step, Volume 1, Olive Hurley
Complete instructions for the most popular ceili dances (video).

Hula for Everyone – Your Complete Hula Lesson
Learn the hula with these easy step-by-step lessons (video/DVD).

Note to parents and teachers: every effort has been made by the Publishers to ensure that these websites are suitable for children, that they are of the highest educational value, and that they contain no inappropriate or offensive material. However, because of the nature of the Internet, it is impossible to guarantee that the contents of these sites will not be altered. We strongly advise that Internet access is supervised by a responsible adult.

Dancing is a fun way to get fit, but like any form of physical exercise it has an element of risk, particularly if you are unfit, overweight or suffer from any medical conditions. It is advisable to consult a healthcare professional before beginning any programme of exercise.

Glossary

Aerobic exercise Exercise that improves breathing and circulation.

Barn dance An English folk dance with a caller.

Caller A person who calls out the moves at a country dance.

Ceilidh/ceili An English, Scottish or Irish social gathering with traditional music, dancing and storytelling.

Contra dancing A type of American folk dancing in which couples face each other in a line.

Dance ranch A venue holding a country and western dance party.

Folk dance A traditional dance originating amongst ordinary people.

Hormone A substance produced by the body, which affects the way the body functions.

Hornpipe A lively folk dance originally accompanied by a woodwind instrument made partly of horn.

Hula A Polynesian dance accompanied by rhythmic drumbeats and chanting.

Isolations A type of exercise involving moving one part of the body without moving the rest.

Jig A lively dance in triple time.

Mazurka A Polish folk dance.

Morris dance A very energetic form of English folk dancing performed by teams dressed in traditional costumes.

Native American A member of any of the aboriginal peoples of the western hemisphere; especially in North America.

Peasants Labourers and small farmers who made up a large proportion of the population in the past.

Polka A lively Polish dance based on three steps and a hop in fast time.

Reel A moderately fast dance from the Highlands of Scotland.

Rhythm The regular sounds in a piece of music.

Square dance A dance in which sets of four couples form squares as they dance the moves.

Tarantella A lively, whirling dance from southern Italy.

Venue A place where people gather to watch or take part in an event.

Zorba A Greek dance, which is usually performed by men.

Index

American dance 2, 8–16, 28

barn dancing 9, 19
bridge of Athlone, the 22–23

callers 9, 11, 17, 19
ceilidhs/ceilis 17–23
    English 18–19
    Irish 17, 22–23
    Scottish 17, 20–21
contra dancing 9
Cossack dance 25
country and western 2, 9, 11
country dancing 8, 19, 21

dance ranches 11
dancewear 5, 8, 20, 21, 24

exercise
    aerobic 2, 4
    body isolations 5
    cool-down 7
    warm-up 4–6

folk dancing 2, 9, 17, 19, 23, 24–29

gay gordons, the 17, 20–21
Greek dance 25

Hawaiian dance 29
Hungarian dance 24–27

Indian dance 29
Irish dance 17, 22–23
Italian dance 25

line dancing 2, 8–16

mazurka, the 25
morris dancing 28, 29
music 2, 5, 10, 16, 17

Polish dance 25

Russian dance 25

Saint Bernard's waltz, the 17, 18–19
square dancing 9

tarantella, the 25
Turkish dance 29

zorba, the 25

First published in 2005 by Franklin Watts,
96 Leonard Street, London EC2A 4XD

Franklin Watts Australia
Level 17/207 Kent Street
Sydney, NSW 2000

Copyright © Franklin Watts 2005

Series editor: Rachel Cooke
Art director: Peter Scoulding

**Series designed and created for Franklin
Watts by STOREYBOOKS Ltd.**
Designer: Rita Storey
Editor: Fiona Corbridge
Photography: Tudor Photography, Banbury
Dance consultant: Lucie-Grace Welsman

Picture credits
Corbis/Ted Streshinsky p.9; Corbis/Sygma p.17;
Corbis/Gail Mooney p.25.

Cover images: Tudor Photography, Banbury.

Every attempt has been made to clear copyright.
Should there be any inadvertent omissions,
please apply to the publisher for rectification.

All photos posed by models.
Thanks to James Boyce, Kimesha Campbell,
Hazel Hathway, Ricky Healey, Aisha Hussain,
Fern Jelleyman, Charlie Storey and Hannah
Storey.

With many thanks to Goody Two Shoes, Rugby,
who supplied all the costumes.

A CIP catalogue record for this book is available
from the British Library.
Dewey number: 792.8
ISBN 0 7496 6348 0
Printed in China